BROKEN SILENCE

Living with Passion and Purpose after Sexual Abuse

A DANCER'S STORY

JEAN DORFF

ONE LESS STORY TO TELL

In BROKEN SILENCE: Living with Passion and Purpose after Sexual Abuse, A Dancer's Story, I tell my story of sexual abuse, the effects it had on my life and how I now thrive instead of just survive. I hope to give others the courage to tell their story and to break the silence too. There are more than 1,000 sexual abuse victims a day. Imagine... that's one per minute. Sexual abuse victims are not nameless. They are not numbers in a report; they are people with a name, with a family, often tainted for the rest of their lives. I believe that there is healing in telling your story. Sexual abuse is still a topic of taboo. By giving abuse a face, we'll bring it out of the dark into the light.

Tell your story too! It will encourage and empower others to do the same...

Go to www.1les2tell.org and tell Your Story So There is ONE LESS STORY TO TELL

1less2tell.org is an initiative from A Dancers's Movement to Stop Sexual Abuse Inc.

Broken Silence: Living with Passion and Purpose after Sexual Abuse

Jean Dorff

Disclaimer

I have tried to recreate events, locales, and conversations from my memories. To maintain anonymity, in some instances, I have changed the names of individuals and places and some identifying characteristics and details.

DEDICATION

I dedicate this book to my precious children, Dièz and Naveen.

To Dièz and Naveen, I love you so much. You never leave my thoughts, and you will always and forever be in my heart. I know I cannot protect you from everything, but I hope and fight with all my might that what I've been through will pass by your lives.

To my siblings, I know you all have your own stories.
I love you dearly.

To all survivors of sexual abuse, my God gave me the strength to write my story and speak on stage and through media. I hope that in some way I also speak for you.

CONTENTS

INTRODUCTION

I would rather be dead than to live longer with this pain and filth in me. I hate myself so much and don't want to be here anymore . . . I want to love and be loved so much . . . but it never works out . . . why why why why why why?

This book is not meant to be a scientific analysis of sexual abuse and domestic violence survival. What I want to achieve is to give an insight to my story. Representing all the survivors is not what I want to (or can) achieve, but I can offer my perspective. Over the years, I've noticed two important things. First, it's helpful for victims to hear the stories of other survivors. Second, there are undeniable commonalities between how I dealt with (and still deal with) day-to-day life issues and how I've seen other survivors dealing with their issues.

WHAT IS THIS BOOK ABOUT?

It is about me, a person who survived sexual abuse and domestic violence. It's how I dealt with it during my younger life and later as an adult.

The intent of this book is to give other survivors the hope and the tools to thrive and not only survive.

The purpose of this book is to draw attention to the cause of sexual abuse; to start a movement so that the number of sexual abuse cases finally decreases and ideally disappears completely.

This book is also about our inner strength, or at least an introduction to the inner-strength method.

- To give insight on how to leverage your past ordeals and turn them into empowerment of oneself and empowerment for others.
- To give insight on growing and enforcing your inner strength by using your five energies to move past your fears and start a life of passion and purpose.

I'm Unbroken

There are 600,000 sexual abuse cases every year in Europe and the United States together. To put it in perspective, that's one new victim every minute. So, before you have finished this page, there will be another few victims. Let's say it takes you three minutes to read one page in this book. That is more than 450 victims before you have the chance to read this book, cover to cover. Almost 100 victims to watch an average movie. That is 1,440 victims every day.

Everyone I speak to says, "This has to stop; every victim is one too many." I agree completely. But why is it that these abuse numbers aren't going down? Instead, these numbers are going up. A careful estimate by several organizations is that 60 to 70 percent of sexual abuse cases go unreported, like my own experience. At least three of my family members were abused by the same uncle, and we never reported it.

Leading up to writing my story, I talked to numerous people about the topic of sexual abuse. The men are shocked and typically don't want to accept, or can't believe, that these numbers are so high.

Men are typically also those who have a grayer definition of what sexual abuse is.

The definition of sexual abuse is simple: **anything done of a sexual nature to another person, physically or mentally, without clear consent of that person is sexual abuse.** If we run the numbers of abuse by this definition, the figures would go through the roof. In other words, no really means no. And where it involves children in the US under the age of eighteen, and in most European countries under the age of sixteen (which is too young, in my mind), it is **always** sexual abuse, with or without the child's consent.

But let me tell you this, I'm not writing this to take revenge on my abusers or expose them. In fact, they have already passed away. You might ask, "Do you write this to raise awareness for sexual abuse and domestic violence?" Yes, although I hope to increase the awareness by publishing this book, I strongly believe that awareness on its own is not nearly enough. If I only count the thousands upon thousands of victims, like myself, it becomes clear that many people are already aware. However, if awareness is not followed by any action or change, not much can be expected to happen to the number of sexual abuse cases. So, it needs to more than awareness, way more for this abuse to go away.

I see seven groups, and each needs to take their responsibility.

1. *Victims need to break their silence.* I know this is not easy. It took me long enough. People will not believe you and they might even turn against you. But there is healing in breaking the silence and, more important, you can prevent other cases from happening.

2. *Parents need to take this more seriously.* They need to be less naïve in thinking this won't happen to their children and be more proactive and informed. I'm sure my parents thought the

same. And the millions of parents with children who are already victims will also testify to that. I wish that we could raise our children in full freedom so that we don't have to warn them about this evil and don't have to train them how to prevent it. But this is too naïve. Remember, 80 percent of the sexual abuse done to children is done by people who know the victim well. In my case, it was close family members.

3. *Men need to take responsibility.* Over 90 percent of the abusers are men. We can and should be the strongest voice in stopping the objectification of women. I'm not taking the moral high ground here. The things I've done could probably not stand the test of this either. Now, I could say I'm a sexual abuse victim; I'm all screwed up. That might be true, but I realize what a messed-up world we live in. Men need to step forward and expose their own shady behavior—addictions to porn, the sick jokes when they are together, how they talk about women. What if it was your daughter in that porn movie? What if it was your daughter who was the subject of the jokes?

4. *Schools, colleges, and universities need to provide safeguards.* The sexual abuse cases in school and especially in higher education institutions are incredibly high. One in four first-year girls have been sexually abused in US colleges. Before you reject this number, just stop for a moment and think about it. My daughter is about to go to college, and I'm so excited for her. But sending her to college is almost more dangerous than sending her to a war zone.

5. *Authorities and politics need to make this issue a priority.* Why are we all aware of the problem and know these numbers, but it never makes it high on political agendas? How come we think we need to fight crime and don't see sexual abuse as one of the evilest crimes we need to fight and ban from this world?

6. *Churches need to openly discuss sexual abuse.* Yes, I'm a Christian and I go to church. But I have to conclude that the number of sexual abuse cases is not different in churches than in other groups. Sex and intimacy is from God, at least that is what I believe. Then tell me, how is it that discussing these topics in churches is so hard? Sex is often seen or portrayed as something bad and evil in religion. Sex is not evil. Sex without mutual consent is evil.

7. *Women need to empower themselves.* Women are by far the largest group victimized by sexual harassment, sexual abuse, and domestic violence. In my work as a life coach and a professional dance coach, I work with women from all walks of life. I haven't met one who wasn't in some way subjected to harassment, abuse, or violence at least once in their lives. Women need to break the silence; stand up; don't let yourselves be victimized. More important, empower yourselves and others to prevent this "disease" from further spreading.

One more thing I want to say here. We all need to break the silence, define with one another what to do, what actions to take, because raising awareness is not enough. **We need to stop sexual abuse and domestic violence for all men, women, and children.**

"You can recognize survivors of abuse by their courage. When silence is so very inviting, they step forward and share their truth so others know they aren't alone. Broken Silence is such a powerful and truthful read for all."

MICHAEL MALITOWSKI AND JOANNA LEUNIS
- Professional Latin Dance Champions.

CHAPTER 1

My Story

What if the ones who should give you protection are the ones you need protection from?

That First Time

It was a hot summer day in July. There was no school and the weather was nice, a little too hot maybe. It was quiet outside. Besides the laughter of playing children, there were almost no sounds. I guess most people tried to find some coolness in the shade or in their houses.

It must have been right after noon when he asked me to follow him upstairs into the bedroom. I was a little nervous and felt the summer heat in the small bedroom. He closed the curtains to keep the sun and the heat out, as he said. From the bedroom window on the second floor, I saw glimpses of my brother and my cousin playing in the backyard. They were outside, and my uncle and I had the time to ourselves. Little chance that we were going to be disturbed.

With a smile, he looked at me and invited me to lay next to him in bed. The bed was too small for two people, but that didn't matter much. He must have known that it was my first time; he didn't rush anything. The softness and saltiness of his lips made me forget where I was. And when I felt his hands all over me, I forgot everything. The sounds outside, the warmth of the summer, it all disappeared. He covered my face with his kisses.

He was gentle. I only heard his voice and the sweet tender sounds of his words, calming me and telling me that it was all ok. It was strange to feel his skin on mine. He hushed me and said, "Let's be real quiet." It was a different "playing" than I expected, but I wanted to trust him, so I nervously followed his lead. His hands were going down, and I started to be afraid. Again, he said that it was all okay, but it didn't feel okay. Maybe because it was all new for me? Maybe because it was daytime, and we were in bed? Maybe because the children from outside could come running in any moment?

Or maybe, just maybe, because I was seven years old and he was my uncle.

This could have been a great start of a romantic story, but there is little romance in my story. It was the summer of 1968, almost fifty years ago, and because one man, my uncle, decided to follow his lust and selfish desires, he changed the course of my life. My uncle, instead of protecting me, was the one I needed protection from.

This was the start of my story of sexual abuse, a word or context that I certainly did not understand at that time. It was the first of countless times that he abused me. Whenever he had the chance to take advantage of me, to use my body for his own pleasures and needs, he did.

THE SECRET AND THE SHAME

You might wonder how something so evil and bad could go on for so long and for so many times. Instead of going to my parents and telling them what happened, I kept it all to myself. I kept it a secret for many years. My uncle told me that he would do something bad to me if I would tell anyone. He convinced me that I was the one doing something wrong, that I would get punished by my parents. He gave me five dollars, as a kind of reward, if I kept my mouth shut.

But it was not only his threats or the money that stopped me from telling what happened. It was more so an immediate feeling of shame, a feeling that I did something wrong, so wrong that I couldn't tell my "secret" to anyone, too afraid that someone would expose my "wrongdoing." On top of that feeling of shame and thinking I did something wrong, I was also afraid that my parents would punish me.

But, unfortunately, by not immediately telling my parents what happened, I enabled my abuser, my uncle, to let him do his things to me until I was about twelve years old.

I wanted to tell someone. I wanted to be saved. I wanted to not be afraid, but I was more afraid of what would happen if someone found out, especially my dad. In hindsight, my dad most likely would have listened to me and protected me. The sad thing is that I didn't grow up in a family where I felt safe to come forward with a story like this.

UNSAFE, WHERE IT SHOULD HAVE BEEN SAFE

I grew up in a big family—three brothers and three sisters. I was the youngest boy and the second youngest child. We were not rich and had to share bedrooms, nothing unusual where we grew up. We had a lot of laughter and joy in the family, always good food on the table. Mom was an excellent cook, and I don't only say that because I'm her son. Our parents insisted on having our dinners together. "At least once a day, we have to sit together," was their motto—a tradition that I still carry on. The table was always properly set, something Mom really cared about. So, all in all, I have mostly good memories of the family dinners, the family get-togethers, and the yearly vacations we shared.

Dad often talked about how important it was for him to keep the family together, no matter what. Born and raised in Indonesia, he grew up in a broken family. Poverty, alcoholism, the war, and a lot of reasons why that brokenness happened in his family. Because of how he was raised and his personal experiences, he had a strong belief that one needed to be tough and disciplined to survive in this world.

He wanted to warn and protect his children from the evil that was out there. One of the things he used to say was, "When you meet someone, start with not trusting this person. You can always change your mind about this person later." He didn't only try to toughen us up mentally, he also tried to physically harden us. Our playing was always tough and hard and more than once we got bruised or worse.

We didn't mind being honest; it was kind of our family thing. I remember at least one instance when a boy from across the street saw how rough we were with one another, and he ran home to tell his mom that we were killing one another. Most of my friends loved my dad. He often took us on day trips to nature areas where we enjoyed survival types of games. There was, however, a dark side in all that "toughening and hardening us."

One day, one of my brothers came home and my dad discovered that he had been in a fight and didn't win. My dad said, "You go out there and beat the other guy up, or else I will beat you up."

Now this might sound like a funny story and perhaps makes a good anecdote today. Unfortunately, the truth is that my dad did beat us up, maybe not on that occasion but he did on so many others. And I'm not talking about a sporadic, correctional spanking. When we did something wrong, he was not shy to take out his belt or something else he could beat us with. He thought he was fair, because he always asked us if we deserved our punishments. If we said yes, he beat us. If we said no, he punished us twice as much, because now we had also lied. If he couldn't figure out who deserved the punishment, he would punish us all.

Some of my siblings still believe that my dad was just and fair and that we deserved the punishments we got, because of the things we did. Others think that he had the best intentions of raising us in the way he thought was right, and that because of how he was raised and what he had been through that he was just tougher than other dads. Good intentions or not, no kids should ever be beaten by their parents in the way my dad did.

My dad was an alcoholic. Most of the time he was able to control his addiction well. I have really bad memories of when he didn't. There was one occasion when we had to use force to get him off one of my brothers, because he said he was going to strangle him. On another instance, we had to take another brother to the hospital after he got cuts in his head, because dad threw a stool at him. I will never forget that time when he stood in front of me with a knife and said to me, "I've put you on this world and I can take you off it too."

I'm sure that my dad regrets this, and I actually hope that he forgot most of it. His war trauma, his own upbringing and abuse, his alcoholism, his adjustment to a new country, and changing times are perhaps all good clarification of his violent behavior, but it created so much stress and fear at home. It caused most of us to also solve our problems with aggression and violence, among one another and toward others.

So, perhaps we had a lot of good moments at home with Dad, probably more good moments than bad ones, however, there was always this tension that circumstances could change quickly, and laughter and joy could turn into anger and domestic violence.

What this did to me was create an unsafe place where I wanted to feel safe. Unfortunately, I hardly ever felt safe when my dad was home. I felt that I had to walk on eggshells all the time. I felt I had to be perfect and was afraid to make mistakes or upset my parents.

More Violence and Another Secret

So, after this story of my uncle sexually abusing me, and growing up in a family where my dad more than just occasionally would beat me, you would think that a young boy's life couldn't be further screwed up. I regret to tell you that you are wrong.

The violence at home, the sexual abuse with my uncle, so often I tried to flee from this. I wanted to be alone, but being alone was fairly hard in my big family. Not only was my dad violent, but also my mom at times could go way beyond a normal spanking. I vividly remember one time that she spanked my brother and me with a rug beater. I had such marks on my legs that I couldn't go to school in shorts for at least a week. In addition, my older brothers' arguments easily turned into serious physical fights. They would hit or throw things at each other. Most of us developed a habit of breaking stuff when we were angry.

My brother, directly above me, is five years older than me. He and I shared the same bedroom, we had to sleep in a small, queen-size bed for most of the time that we shared the room. I don't know how it started, but more than once he asked me to do things under the blanket, so to speak. We were ten and fifteen years old when these things happened.

I know now how wrong this was but unlike with my uncle, I never hated my brother for this. It only shows how screwed up things really were. I know that my brother knew about my uncle's sexual abuse of me. More than once he called me a "faggot." The other thing I knew, or at least strongly suspected, was that he also was a victim of my uncle. Later in life when I tried to talk to him about this, he always became angry, ran away, and said that he didn't want to talk about this ever. My brother passed away a few years ago, and we never had a chance to talk about this. Recently I found out, through his wife, that he indeed was abused by the same uncle, and also by others.

Looking back on this, I never felt any anger or hate for my parents or my brother. That doesn't mean that I think what happened was okay. Emotionally I don't feel that way.

What I do feel is utter disgust at how things in young people's lives, like my siblings and me, can get so screwed up. I call this chapter "My Story," but you see now it is not only my story. All my siblings lived through a life with an extreme, dominant dad. I know that I was not the only victim of my uncle's sexual abuse. So, this could easily have been my siblings' story too—and that's only accounting for one family.

Every day, thousands of stories like mine start. Young kids are harmed by growing up in a family with violence and abuse. Sometimes it's just a single event, sometimes it's a long period of abuse and violence. The consequences of these events deeply scar the lives of those who are affected for the rest of their lives.

Although each story is unique, the outcome for the lives of sexual abuse and domestic violence victims is similar. The results are too often a messed-up life with a long struggle to find balance, a hard time to maintain good and deep relationships, and the ongoing search to have confidence, to feel self-worth, and to go through life with trust, free from fear, with a sense of freedom.

CHAPTER 2

THE BROKENNESS STARTS TO SHOW

The early impact and my teen years.

Shame

Alone

Fatalism

Guilt

So, there I was a young child, dealing with stuff I now can see that children should not have to deal with. At the time, however, I didn't know better. This was my world, one where I felt unsafe and often alone. I frequently heard my parents or my siblings say, "Oh, Jean? Yes, he is often by himself reading books, and when he reads a book he doesn't hear or see anything else." Well, that's exactly one of the reasons why I was reading books, to escape, like I also did in movies, if I had the chance.

Things were not only bad, of course not. Far from it, if you would measure it in time. In fact, you can easily write off the things I've been through as a "few" incidents. You can even say that when it comes to my dad, he actually tried to raise us the best way he thought possible.

He strongly believed that the world was evil and hard and that the only way to survive was to be incredibly tough.

However, the impact of the domestic violence I endured went beyond the physical. I learned in life that no matter how good a person is or *no matter how well the intentions were, it doesn't make right what is wrong*. I don't hold a grudge against my father, not at all. But the relationship is broken, and it's sometimes hard to find love for him.

When it comes to my uncle, there is no way I can see that he had a reason or a motive for his actions, at least not one that I could possibly understand. I think he was just a lust-driven predator. I know he was also a father and husband. I don't know what his story is, but for sure he would have a story to tell too. In the end, it's what he did to this world and not his motives or his history that count. His story could give us insight about why he did what he did. But no matter what his story was, it doesn't take away the damage he caused.

As a young person, I had no clue how I was damaged by the sexual abuse and the domestic violence. Things were just as they were, and I had little or no reference, at least not consciously, how things could or would have been different if I grew up in other circumstances. It's also hard to define how my character would have developed if things had been different for me.

So often, later in life, I tried to get answers to these questions, perhaps knowing that I would never get them. Reading and hearing other victim's stories gave me the insight that victims develop a similar internal world and outward behavior as I did.

The brokenness I felt started to show up early. I was mostly a withdrawn kid. Reading was an escape and a way to shut out the world. I guess that's what I tried to do most of the time—shut out the world. If I didn't have a rich fantasy already, then for sure I developed one. I liked to fantasize about different worlds and escape into them, if only with my thoughts.

I was insecure and afraid about many things, although it never seemed that way to others, because I was a relatively popular kid at school and among my friends. I was, however, insecure and tried always so hard to fit in, to be acknowledged and to be seen. The way I solved it was also to take leadership and try to become exceptional in at least one area. In my case, it was first in martial arts, later in my work and dance.

I Am the Only One

Although sexual abuse victims know that they are not the only victims, they often feel alone in their pain. Either they have never shared what they have been through and/or they believe that they have to deal with it all by themselves. This isolation is often fed by shame, the will to keep it a secret, guilt, or thinking there is no support for them. In all cases, this limiting belief hinders sexual abuse victims from moving forward and finding healing.

The South Eastern Centre Against Sexual Assault & Family Violence (www.secasa.com.au) describes it like this.

> Feelings of differentness, alienation, isolation and despair are often experienced by sexual assault survivors if they are unable to share their experiences with others. Societal norms prevent many victims from speaking out about their experience of sexual assault and many victims, women in particular, have few avenues for personal communication. This is particularly the case for victims assaulted by their partners or acquaintances.

Sexual abuse is in most cases (80 percent or higher) done by someone close, often someone the victim trusted. I was abused by an uncle, a close family member. This deep violation of trust had a deep impact on how I started to see people. Until that point, I believed I lived in a world that was safe, where I could rely on the people around me. That was over with one act of abuse and was violated repeatedly in the years after that by my uncle and other abusers.

I am always shocked to hear how many victims believe they are the only victim of their abusers. Isolation is another tactic that child abusers use. They put a lot of pressure on their victims by threatening them that more bad things will happen if they ever tell anyone. They bribe their victims by rewarding them if they keep "abuse" secret. This cycle of threats and rewards creates a complete mental dependency of the victim by the abuser. This is seen a lot in domestic violence and abuse cases and causes more isolation of the victim.

This belief that victims have to solve their problems alone and that they have to carry the burden by themselves can drive them to complete isolation. It becomes a problem when victims try to build new relationships. It can lead to depression, even suicide. In all cases, it hinders the victims from moving forward and healing.

I can really relate to this. Besides the shame and guilt, I was also afraid of what my parents would say or do. When the abuse was going on, I was mostly afraid of the physical punishment my parents would give me. My abuser convinced me to keep it a secret—not only would my parents be angry at me, but they would also punish me.

I was afraid that people would find out, so I started to keep the truth to myself. To keep this secret for so many years was mentally a heavy burden for me. Furthermore, I started to keep most things to myself. In hindsight, as extroverted as I am, this caused many problems, specifically in the relationships I had.

It Is What It Is (Fatalism)

Sexual abuse victims, especially those who have been abused over a longer period of time, develop a perception that the situation they were (or are) in cannot be changed. Their cry for help has for too long been unheard or fully neglected. Because of this, they keep this false belief that things are the way they are and cannot be changed.

Oftentimes, a sexual abuse victim is not a victim on only one occasion. The abuse can stretch out over a number of years and be done by multiple abusers. More than once, victims find themselves trapped in a cycle of abusive relationships later in life. So, they come to the belief that they are enslaved in a circle of bad fate they can't escape. This acceptance of their "fate" can turn into fatalism, where the abuse victims believe that they no longer have control over their situations and their lives.

When abuse victims end up being repeatedly in "wrong" relationships, they also develop a belief that they have no ability to make right decisions in life. This strengthens the conviction of the sexual abuse victim that things are as they are and cannot be changed.

In my own case, the abuse started at the age of seven. The wrongdoing went through my puberty, with more than one abuser. I started to accept these things as a given and a stroke of fate. I finally found a way to overcome this, but I now know that many victims are not that fortunate.

This limiting belief that life situations cannot be changed hinders sexual abuse victims to move on and to heal.

We often say, "Things are as they are" or "It is what it is." Well, maybe so, but to just accept that what happens to you as a fait accompli is just not right and definitely not the right thing to do. Unfortunately, as human beings we'll get used to everything. Or in my case, I really started to develop the feeling and idea that I could not change the situation I was in. I tried to prevent it, and I'm sure I was successful many times, but when I was in a situation where the abuse took place, I just let it come over me. I often just let it happen and hoped that when I obeyed and did what was asked of me, it would be over soon. I'm an empathetic person, but my empathy was turned so often to apathy.

It's My Own Fault (Guilt)

A belief that sexual abuse victims often develop is the belief that what has happened to them was their own fault. That in some twisted way, they are responsible for what has overcome them. Victims often build this huge complex of guilt; this limiting belief hinders them to move on, to seek sexual abuse counseling, and to heal. This belief and guilt can be especially strong when the abuser was someone close, like a friend, a family member, or even a spouse or partner.

It is often hard for sexual abuse victims to accept that someone so close would do something so bad to them. Consumed by the question why, victims are looking for faults in their own behaviors. During the investigation of rape, investigators question the victims if they were dressed appropriately or whether their behaviors triggered reactions of any kind of nature that made a wrong emotion that would have "seduced" the rapist. This kind of questioning only builds the doubt and guilt victims already have.

For abused young children, their abusers often want to give them the feeling that it is their fault, especially when the abuse is paired with violence. In the case of childhood sexual abuse, abusers make children believe that they deserve the "punishments" they received. Receptive as children are to adult's influence, abused children easily develop this sense of guilt, and they can carry it with them for a long time.

In my own case, my abuser offered me money. I was seven years old and had no conception of what he was going to do to me. There was, however, an immediate feeling that I did something wrong. Because I was forced into something that was wrong and accepted money for it, guilt started to develop from the beginning. In their need for an answer, sexual abuse victims sometimes question their own behaviors or whether they clearly said no to their abuser.

For victims, it is never a joke. How often did I scream, "NO," but nobody responded to my desperate cries? The needed response definitely did not come from my abuser, whose only aim was to satisfy his lust and needs. In hindsight, I sometimes ponder how I ever could have believed that this was my fault.

It is almost incomprehensible that victims can have this strong feeling of guilt. Unfortunately, this is one of the beliefs that victims have, a false belief that is strongly rooted, a belief that limits them to move forward. It's apparent that victims have to overcome this limiting belief, like I did, to get the necessary healing from what has happened, like I received.

It's perhaps a little bit harder for adults to understand why a child can believe that he or she gave cause for another person to act on. But some children are raised when every time something happened or went wrong their parents asked, "What did you do?" As if it was automatically assumed that the child did something wrong. Hence the feeling of "It's my own fault" was already in me before the abuse started.

In cases where older kids or adults are abused, that feeling of "It's my own fault" can be even greater. Remember, over 80 percent of abuse is done by someone the victim knows well. In the instances where rape and abuse cases are investigated, more than often the interrogators, by the way questions are asked, give victims the feeling that they gave cause to the event of abuse and rape. It's almost needless to state what this does to the victim's mindset.

The abuser in almost all cases accuses the victim. After the abusive act, physical and/or verbal, the abuser often blames the victim, out of the abuser's own feelings of guilt, anger, and rage.

I Need to Keep It a Secret (Shame)

Regardless of how old or how young we are, consciously we never like to go out in the open and share or confess what we have done wrong. In the case of sexual abuse, it would be what victims believe they did wrong or the belief that they did something shameful. This often causes abuse victims to keep what happened to themselves.

In all sexual abuse cases, this limiting belief that it is better to keep it a secret, hinders the healing process. It is a huge factor for the victim to move forward and to seek the needed help in healing. Some of the most common reasons why sexual abuse victims keep their secrets are as follows

- They are being forced or threatened.
- They believe that it's less real.
- They are ashamed of the acts.
- They want to protect others.

It is obvious why it is in the best interest of the perpetrators to keep their deeds secret. They often threaten or bribe their victims just to ensure they keep silent about it. And mostly, it is out of angst and heavy repercussion that the victims keep quiet about what happened to them.

This is especially true for young victims. They often think that if they stay silent about these terrible events, the events were not real. It is so hard for abuse victims to fathom that someone did this to them, that instead they build a belief of a different reality or suppress the memory.

For the same reason, they don't tell others because they convinced themselves already that no one believes them anyhow.

Sexual abuse victims are often loaded with shame over what has happened to them. They are willing to suffer by themselves rather than relating and sharing the story to a concerned party. They create this belief that the shame would get even bigger if they shared their story. For men, specifically, it is often hard to admit that they were intimate with another man; that it was against their will doesn't matter.

Another reason is a twisted one. Victims at times think that they are protecting others by not telling their stories. In my case, I always believed that I would protect my parents by not telling what happened to me. I never wanted a shade of shame to come over my family, and I also never wanted to give my parents the feeling that they were not able to protect me.

But maybe even more twisted and perhaps the hardest one for victims to deal with is the feeling that they partly enjoyed the abuse. I would lie if I would say that all the things done to me by my uncle felt bad or painful. At times, I did like the way he touched me, the way he gave me attention, and how he made me feel special. Admitting this and writing it was hard for me, and the feeling of being ashamed came up big when I did.

The longer victims keep their secrets, the harder it is for them to share. They make themselves believe that those are distant memories. Likewise, they adhere and conclude that no good can possibly come from telling it to someone after all this time. The unfortunate fact is that keeping it a secret is one of the biggest hindrances for sexual abuse victims to move forward and to heal.

The One Thing That Changed Everything

The abuse and domestic violence continued until I was about twelve years old. Most of my siblings left the house and things were much nicer at home, with the exception of some events, but those are irrelevant to this story.

The things done to us leave deep scars. Over the years, I discovered I had many. *I hope my scars now tell a story that helps other people to heal.*

I was afraid at night and tried to hush every discussion at home that had the potential to escalate into an argument and turn into physical violence. By the time I was seventeen, I had created my own world. A world that basically was run by "keeping the peace" in all situations. For instance, I made sure that my parents were never upset with me. I loved my parents for so many things, but I was also afraid of them, especially my dad.

One day, as my mind wandered back to that summer day when the abuse started, I felt anger and hatred. But something was different this time . . . I just felt that things had to change. I didn't want my life to be run by anger and hate; we had enough of that in my family. Something came over me—forgiveness for my uncle. There was nothing logical about it, and I was actually fighting that feeling of forgiveness, as if I wanted to hang on to the anger and hate. As unbelievable as it might sound, it was a conscious decision to forgive my abuser, not driven by reason and rationale but by heartfelt emotions.

The forgiveness changed everything, but forgiveness is not a one-time event. It is a continuous process and only a first step of all phases anyone needs to go through to heal from sexual abuse. I will tell all about these phases in later chapters.

I don't believe my uncle had any regrets for what he did. That makes him probably one of the evilest people I've ever met. To find forgiveness for him had little to do with him but more so with forgiving myself. My sister, who never found forgiveness for my uncle, is still dealing with this.

With the forgiveness for my uncle, it felt like a huge weight was lifted off my shoulders. I felt more freedom and stepped into the world more positive and closer to my core.

I would love to tell you that after this everything was fine and that I lived only a happy life. But although I believe that forgiveness is a huge part of healing from sexual abuse, it is not the only step, and healing is not a one-time event. It's a process of many, maybe endless, small steps.

CHAPTER 3

SEARCH FOR THE
ULTIMATE GOOD

At a young age, I started to develop a strong feeling that people could not be fully trusted, thinking they would hurt me in the end anyhow. I felt alone and fled into a world of thoughts and fantasies. I always had walls around me, and I became a master of masking them. While I tried to fit into the "normal" world by doing normal stuff and following the rules, I also searched for love, understanding, and acceptance.

Trying to find my own identity and a place in a world that so often didn't make sense to me, I grew up as a serious kid who spent hours by myself reading, thinking, and daydreaming. I remember that I always hoped something great would happen, something that would change the world and make it pretty and friendly.

I fell in love with movies, especially musicals and fantasy movies. I dreamed of being a dancer, like Fred Astaire, or a hero who changed the world. I read books about spirituality and foreign religions, hoping that I would find answers to questions I didn't even understand.

In my mind, I lived a creative, colorful life. In real life, I was a conformist, trying to please others and afraid to bend rules too far. In my first marriage, I felt older than I am now. A passionless relationship with my high school girlfriend, I was too afraid of letting her go and that no one else would love me again. I also spent half a lifetime studying martial arts. Although it brought me great knowledge, skills, and success, I always tried to be more macho than I really was, or am.

My career went fairly well. Through evening studies and hard work, I worked my way up to a business strategist and marketeer specialized in educational global markets. But if I look critically back on all this, I felt out of place in the corporate arena. I was more driven by pleasing my bosses and trying to meet the expectations of my reference groups than by true intrinsic motivation.

My life with my second wife had many highs and some serious lows. In the first part of our relationship, before we got married, I didn't take being truthful and faithful to each other too seriously. During the few breaks we had, I was trying to prove something by dating as many women as I possibly could. None of this gave me true satisfaction. But when my second wife and I made a serious commitment to our relationship, I started to feel more content and happier, more than I was before. We discovered competitive, Latin American dancing. We started late in age, but we did reasonably well with reasonable results, perhaps against all expectations.

In dancing, I found my passion but sadly approached it from the point of view of a conformist. I wanted to be like "dancer so and so," or be a good representative of our dance school, not disappointing our teachers. I never dared to approach dancing as an expression of myself. I analyzed dancing as I had analyzed the world as a young kid. I watched it from the outside and never from the inside.

Again, I was more obsessed with doing it right and afraid of failures and mistakes. I'm sure I pained my partner many times with this obsessive behavior. What she perhaps didn't know is that I also hurt myself, finding my passion but not living it. In teaching dance, I found joy and a lot of myself, but I didn't take this as a sign to further explore, discover, learn, and go deeper. What I didn't know then is that *finding your passion is different from living your passion.*

About the age of forty-four, things started to change rapidly for me. I thought I was perfectly happy with our life. With two lovely children, a long wish for both of us was fulfilled. We took the opportunity to move to the US for a few years, also something I always wanted.

But something inside me started to change. I felt more depressed and my childhood memories of "living in fear" came to haunt me. I went to my lowest point in life I'd been so far, to a point that brought me to my knees and left me doing the only thing I felt I could do to save myself from taking a drastic step . . . I prayed and cried for help. I couldn't go on like this I wanted to get rid of the pain and had to know what the purpose of my life was.

I prayed to God and, to my own surprise, he spoke to me, at least that is what I believe. I received answers—vivid and clear—over the course of a few weeks. I wrote them down, but that's a different story. Relevant for this story is what I did with the directions God gave me for my life's purpose. I did nothing, nothing more besides writing them down, reading them periodically, and hoping more things would happen or unfold.

I truly believe that I received revelations and insights from my higher power, but it still wasn't enough to put me into motion. I was still waiting for more clues or signs . . . hoping that my life miraculously would change into something better. I found out the hard way that it doesn't. *If you don't put insights, revelations, dreams, whatever you want to call them, into actions, it is totally meaningless.*

At the age of almost fifty, my life had to drastically change another time. My world was crushed when my wife left me with our kids. In the midst of pain, chaos, grief, and confusion, I met a wonderful person who is now my partner, kindred soul, and a true blessing. She heard me talking to others about finding our passions and fulfilling our life's purpose. This probably prompted her to ask me what my deepest passion and dream was. She asked me what I would do if anything was possible. She brought me to a breaking point, and things became shockingly clear for me . . . I was living a life of lies.

I had known what my passion was and perhaps my life's purpose for a long time. I didn't take the clues and directions given to me. I didn't use them to take action.

I also felt thankful, empowered, and excited while at the same time rest came over me and my eyes opened. As if I suddenly understood why I had to go through what I had to go through as a child, as an adolescent, and as an adult. I also understood that there is no such thing as "too late" to follow your passion. But most of all, I knew that I had to take action.

Everybody has a story and you have read mine. Whether we feel compelled to make changes to our lives is up to each individual. We all have to overcome ordeals and pains and live with them. They shape us to what we are today, as mine have shaped me. If they block you from what you want to be, then that is something you can choose to change. If you use them as an excuse to not change, then that is a choice too. But *if you want to change, realize that you have to accept first what you are today before you can become who you want to be tomorrow.*

At the age of fifty-one, I decided to use what I've gone through in life as assets to reach my goals. My experiences are no longer excuses to keep me away from achieving them. I accepted the Lord's grace and let my faith and passion be the driving force to fulfill my life's purpose.

I know now that I haven't been true to myself and perhaps to the people around me for a long time. It's not enough to know what our passion or destiny is. It is actually meaningless until we take action and start walking the path to our life purpose. *It's not about creating a new beginning, it's about creating different endings.*

LIVING A LIFE IN SHADOWS

I doubt if all the mistakes and bad things in life can be blamed on the fact that I was sexually abused and grew up in a family of domestic violence. There is actually no way to tell how my life would have been, if these things didn't happen in my life. My mind often wandered in that direction, but it has little use. If I were to continue thinking about this, it probably hinders my healing more than it does any good.

But we can see from research and stories from victims that they all struggle mentally. Because of that, they have a harder time to live life to the fullest. Even if we set aside the physical impact the abuse has on the victim's life.

For an extrovert like me, who craved so much contact with others, to live a life where I felt that nobody could really be trusted was conflicting and confusing. In my head, I heard my dad reinforcing one of his life's mottos, "Start with distrusting people. You can always trust them later." I concluded that this was a really bad way of approaching and connecting with people.

The problem was not to make new connections. I'm easy with people in all circumstances. The problem is to create deeper connections, especially with the one you live with daily. I had a hard time to give myself fully to a relationship. It seems I did all the right things—talk about emotions, be attentive, provide, etc. At least I believed I did all the right things. At the same time, it scared me to give myself completely, both mentally and physically, no matter how much I wanted to, but I never fully could.

So, I started to create several boxes, like several different lives. One box was where I connected with people more spiritually, another box was where I was outgoing and partying. I had an athletic box where I became a high-level martial artist, and there were many others. Keeping everything in a box gave me a sense of control and safety. It is what I did as an abused kid.

So, from a young age on, I fled into boxes, movies, fantasies, and books. Most of the boxes were not so bad, but there were a few that I'm less proud to talk about. I call them *shadow boxes*. Boxes I didn't want anyone to know about: the secret relationships, the heavy drinking, the sex clubs. I'm sure most people have their secrets and shadow boxes, and I started to notice that our family had many. I also started to notice that other victims had theirs too.

Men generally tend to create boxes in their lives. Apparently abuse enforces this tendency. What this all means is that an abuse victim has a hard time to create a holistic and connected life. This is exactly what my wife always felt; I was not a fully connected partner.

Dancing helped me to see and feel things more from a holistic point of view, but I will have to save that for a later point.

THE SHADOW LIFE

After high school, I decided to find a job and continued to study in the evening. I left my parent's house at the age of eighteen to live together with my high school sweetheart. We had dated off and on since we were sixteen, and we married when I was twenty-one. Unfortunately, the marriage didn't last longer than a year. I felt empty in that relationship and even old. I guess we both didn't really understand what it was to create a loving relationship.

This was different when I met my second wife, although we waited for ten years to get married. We led a passionate life. This relationship was not easy, maybe relationships never are. I basically had no clue what a deep relationship was. We didn't fight much, but when we did, my first reaction was always to run away, break the relationship, telling her that I didn't need her, didn't need anyone. It took me a long time to see there was a pattern there, although I didn't relate it immediately to my abuse history.

Outwardly, I think we had a normal life with our struggles, as we assumed every couple had. We both had good work and our careers went well. We picked up dancing, as I explained previously. But in me grew this hunger for bodily attention. The intimate life between me and my partner was really good, but still it was never enough for me. At first, I started to have affairs outside the relationship. Struggling with integrity, I confessed when I had them. I'm not sure why she stayed with me, but she did. I had to find another way to still this hunger.

Yes, I should have recognized this as unhealthy, but I didn't. Instead, I let my craving drive me into a life of shadows and secrecy. Porn never did it for me. Instead, I went for paid sex, visiting sex clubs and brothels for years. It took a lot out of me to just write this; it's definitely not an episode I'm particularly proud of. I hardly told this to anyone; what I did instead was keeping the shame alive. First, it was the shame of the abuse, next, it started to be the shame of an unquenchable thirst for physical attention.

It was not only the shame that I had paid for sex. I also had a hard time reconciling this with my personal beliefs and standards. So, I truly started to beat myself up, almost daily.

It took me a while to see that I just transformed one personal ordeal into something else—something to keep my mind busy, something to worry about. Another thing that kept me out of living to the fullest; another thing to lie about.

I started to see other things too. People, especially those who are abused, whether physically or mentally, are doing all kind of things to numb their pain. The thing is, most victims don't even know they do it for that reason. They often develop a tendency toward addiction, substance abuse or other obsessions.

Abused people all have shadow lives. The abuse doesn't justify it and isn't an excuse for what I did in my shadow life, neither is it for other victims. So, I don't tell it for that reason. The reason why I tell this part of my story is to make you see that the impact of abuse goes deep and touches many, if not all, aspects of a victim's life.

I can't say it often enough—it would be too easy to use the abuse as an excuse for my behavior in the past, present, or future. But we cannot deny that the behavior we see from abuse victims shows too many similarities to neglect it.

To summarize, on top of the pain (physically, mentally, and emotionally) that a sexual abuse victim has, the long-term impact and struggle goes much deeper and affects all aspects of the victim's life. It also affects more people than just the victim.

CHAPTER 4

FIVE STAGES VICTIMS GO THROUGH

Healing from sexual abuse can take years. Sexual abuse victims have to work themselves through several phases. It seems that the sequence I went through is also what most abusers go through, at least phases one through four.

1. *Accept that you are a victim of abuse.* Acknowledge and remember your sexual abuse. Gain an awareness that your life is driven by past experiences.

2. *Understand your story.* Understand what happened and the pain is big and confusing. Anxiety, low self-worth, fear, and mistrust are part of your world.

3. *Stop being a victim.* You are able to tell your story without getting too overwhelmed by it anymore, at least most of the time. Your abuse history is not controlling your life anymore, but it still gets hold of you from time to time.

4. *Move on.* Without minimizing what has happened to you, you're no longer caught up in your sexual abuse story, and you can look at it with more distance.

5. *Thrive.* Leverage your passion to create the life you want on your terms.

1. Accept That You Are a Victim of Abuse

Acceptance of being a victim of abuse is the start to healing. Therefore, you first need to understand what sexual abuse is. Feeling guilty and feeling ashamed are often reasons why victims cannot fully accept and move on.

Deep inside, victims often believe that they are partly, if not totally, responsible for what has happened to them. Often this guilt or shame is implanted by either the abuser or by others.

Sometimes victims cannot completely remember what has happened to them. Traumatic experiences can lead to memory loss. You might think that it is a good thing, if you don't remember what has happened, especially if they are awful, shocking experiences. The thing is the victim might not exactly remember what has happened, but it is still a memory in an unconscious part of the mind. It's like a toxic poison in people's mind and causes responses like anxiety and deep fears. Not knowing what the cause is leads to significant problems for the victim. Other studies show that all sexual victims exactly remember what has happened, but that they make themselves believe, often out of shame, fear, and guilt, that they don't remember it.

Whatever the effect on the victims, it amounts to the same thing: a derailed emotional life with more consequences than I have time to discuss in this book.

My sister claimed that she had a hard time remembering what really happened between her and our uncle. She only knows that she was raped. One of my coaching clients remembered, more than twenty years later, that she escaped an attempted rape. Although this was painful for her, it gave her much relief, and she felt that things cleared up for her. On the other hand, I always believed that I had clear memories of what happened to me. But it was not until I started writing this book that I discovered more memories of the events happened to me.

I don't believe that it's healthy to go over and over our stories and keep digging into memories that are better forgotten. It is, however, also my belief that acceptance of what has happened is a crucial first step on the way to overcome sexual abuse. Remembering and accepting your story will help end your denial. Allowing yourself to remember is a way of confirming that you didn't just imagine it and is the start of the process of healing. A complete awareness of what has happened gives answers of present behavior and makes victims see that they are driven by past events.

I know I write it and say this often: "I won't let my past experiences be an excuse of my current behavior." But I know now that this is not a realistic point of view. Well, that's to say that if we have a full awareness and understanding of our own story, we can make choices free from events that have happened to us.

2. Understand Your Story

Being aware of your own story, or in other words knowing what has happened, is not the same as understanding your own story.

I was in a car accident. I basically woke up in an ambulance. The awareness of what happened to me brought me to a state of shock. It was only after I recovered from this that I started to put the puzzle pieces together about what had happened to me.

In the process of recovering from sexual abuse, there is a lot of similarity to what I described about the car accident. Most victims are well aware of what happened to them. Completely understanding what has happened is a whole different thing. Again, to know your story and to understand it are two different things: it is more about a sequence of the steps you need to go through.

A vast majority of sexual abuse and domestic violence victims suffer greatly from anxiety, fear, low self-worth, and mistrust. For a smaller group, this has taken proportions to an extent that a "normal" life has become practically impossible. Understanding where conditions such as low self-esteem come from is instrumental in the healing process of the victim. Just remembering the events doesn't necessarily create cognition of the link between present behavior and past experiences.

In my case, it was almost opposite, but the result was the same. My refusal to let my past determine my present behavior didn't allow me to link the two. It was only when I started to work with a therapist and coaches that I had a better understanding of what happened to me. I stayed too long in just "knowing my story," but that didn't help me move fully to a more thriving way of living.

For the longest time, when I thought back to what happened to me, it felt like it was not me. Even when I talked about it, I saw this little boy who had terrible things done to him. But I didn't feel it was me. I believe that you fully need to understand and accept your own story, bring it closer to yourself, before you can take distance from it.

Here are some suggestions to help you tell your story in phases.

- *Tell it first with distance,* often in the third person, as if it didn't really happen to you but to someone else. I often tell it as if it happened to a boy who was not me.

- *Then tell it with the realization that it was you.* The walls of denial come down. It's then when we start really reliving the events.

- As we start to *embody the victim,* we become more wholesome again. It was only when I told my story from a first-person perspective, to say things as they were for me, how I felt them, not as a report of events, that I started to feel a shift.

- We also have to *embody the abusers.* The abuser is not a fictional person, he or she is a real person, an individual often close to us with a personal life. This is essential, and it took me a while to see how important that was. I tried to avoid it, and because I did not have so much contact with my uncle, it was a little easier to picture him as the perpetrator. But most of the time, that is the only way I see him. To fully understand what is going on, I had to see him as a family man, as a man with a life besides what he did that affected me and who knows how many more people. As victims we often want to protect the abusers—after all, if we expose them, then we expose ourselves too. The abuser wants us to think that way. If your abuser is even closer to you, like your sibling or a parent, you start to see them as two different personalities . . . one that violates you, abuses you, gives you pain, and cannot be trusted. But you want to love them, so you create this other personality who can be loved . . . it's complex and it makes me sick writing it. So often, abusers have been abused themselves . . . that makes their abusive acts not better, but it is abundantly clear that we have to stop these cycles. You can read more about my uncle (one of my abusers) at the end of this section.

- *Express your fears.* I grew up as a boy who was afraid of many things—perhaps caused by the abuse and domestic violence. I was afraid of being alone; afraid of being in the dark; afraid of many critters, like spiders; afraid of pain, conflicts, and being wrong. I mostly hid my fears well, but expressing your fears, especially those related to or as a result of your story, is hugely instrumental in the healing process. My biggest fears were these: First, no one can be fully trusted and at some point, everyone will hurt you, something I sometimes still deal with; Second, I was always afraid that I would become an abuser myself, if not sexual then in another sense, for the longest time this was the reason for not wanting to have kids; Third, I had a fear to be left out, to not be accepted for who I was, ultimately the fear of not being loved. Perhaps I became screwed up in some areas, but

I made different choices, hopefully the best ones, and I found strength to step into this world and look for a good life, despite my fears.

Telling your story is one thing. For abuse victims to tell their stories is not an easy thing. One day you might find it easy to tell, while on other occasions you don't even get past the first words. But telling your story is an important step in the healing process. You should tell your story to heal, not to ask for attention, not to victimize yourself (although you are a victim), and certainly not to become your story. Telling your story is ultimately to become free from your story.

Listening to a victim's story is not easy either. If you are not a victim but want to support them, then you should not force victims to tell their stories. Create an environment that feels safe to allow them to reveal it at their own pace. As a listener, be a good listener. To be a good listener is to listen only and not more. The only thing you want to do as a listener is let the other person know that you believe him or her, no matter how ugly the story is.

My Uncle

My uncle's name was Roy. I talk about him in the past tense because he has passed away. Roy was the youngest sibling of my mother. I have few memories of him other than the abuse. The most vivid memory is the first time he abused me, which I described previously.

I remember meeting him again when I was in my late thirties at my grandma's (his mother) funeral. He walked toward me with a big smile, as if he was really happy to see me. I told him that I was there for my grandma. I give him my condolences out of respect for her. I also said to him that he knew why I didn't want to have anything to do with him. I felt strong and was proud of myself to not be either so angry or totally afraid. That was years ago, but I still feel hugely triggered by writing it here.

I once had a strong feeling that I connected with him years after he passed away. Whether this was real, I leave that to you to decide. It felt real to me. I was able to talk to him. I asked him why and if he regretted what he had done to me, to my siblings, and who knows how many more children. He said he didn't regret it at all; it was just what he wanted. I was so disappointed and sad.

You see, deep inside I wanted to believe that my uncle was not all bad, that he had remorse. But I really had to learn and understand that even if that were the case (that he had remorse and regrets for what he did), it wouldn't undo what he had done. I learned not to create feelings of hate or revenge but to take the first step of accepting what happened. Despite this, I found forgiveness in my soul, and that forgiveness is an act of healing the soul, freeing it from toxic thoughts.

As I mentioned previously, seeing abusers as real people and not only as perpetrators is hard but also important on the path of healing.

3. STOP BEING A VICTIM

Knowing and accepting that you are a victim is different from victimizing yourself. The latter has more to do with you consciously and subconsciously using your story to fulfill one or more personal needs.

When you are able to tell your story without getting too overwhelmed by it, at least most of the time, and your abuse history is not controlling your life anymore, even if it still gets a hold of you from time to time, then you are no longer in a victim role.

When I first started telling my stories, I got a lot of compassionate remarks. People genuinely felt for me. They were angry for me; they cried for me. It felt good to tell my story and it relieved me, but it also did something else. I got attention, people were genuinely interested in me or at least in the story. It set me apart, in a more "positive and caring" way and I liked it. Telling my story catered directly to a few of the basic human needs, the need to be significant and the need for attention.

We'll talk more about the healing effects of telling your story, but there is another side of telling your story. To heal fully we also need to be able to recognize that side.

At first, when you tell your story, you relive what you have been through. To some extent you always will. But the more you tell it, the more distance you can take from the actual events. If you don't talk about what happened, it is as if things start to live inside you. It's as if there is something lurking in the shadow, and it comes out at the most unexpected moments. Telling your story will put what you've been through into the light and that's where it can heal.

In my coaching practice, I use a method called shadow light integration, which directly goes to this point. You don't have to talk about your past all the time (the shadows), but as an abused victim, it will serve you well if you can talk about your story (in the light) without getting triggered every time you tell it. That doesn't mean that you will never get triggered, just less often, and when you do get triggered, you know what to do. It's my belief that when you are able to do that, you also stop being a victim. Telling your story is an essential step in the healing process.

4. MOVE ON

When you are able to look at your past with more distance in such a way that you can talk about it without being emotionally triggered, you are ready to move on. Notice that I don't say when you are able to forget your story. If there were a pill that could permanently erase the stories from my memory and take away the pain, then I would take it.

I often hear that from victims—that they are looking for something that takes away the memory and the pain. Unfortunately, that is not how it works. In all reality, no matter how bad our past was, it also makes us who we are today. Could you have been someone else, if these things hadn't happened to you? We don't know for sure and never will. I personally went through that scenario often. I tried to pretend how I would have been without the abuse.

Remarkably enough, I came up with a list of things that I can still pursue. Like being more confident, building stronger relationships, having less fear, connecting more, etc. Sure, these things might be harder for abuse victims, but we can acquire them. So, there is nothing wrong with imagining a life as if you were not a victim, a life with a purpose to discover what you want or don't want.

5. THRIVE

Abuse and domestic violence victims are often already happy if they go through phase four of the healing process. And why wouldn't they be? After all, they have found a way to cope with what is often an ugly history and bad experiences. From my own experience, I want to tell and teach that life is not meant to just go by. Life thoroughly needs to be lived with passion and with purpose.

One of the major discoveries I made, in all my years of talking to survivors and being one myself, is that sexual abuse and domestic violence victims think that thriving in life, leading a life of passion, is not for them. They sometimes believe it's not meant to be, they just don't know how to get there, or they even believe there is no better life for them.

The next chapter goes deeper into how to thrive instead of just survive after sexual abuse and domestic violence.

When I was seeing a psychologist to deal with my abuse history, she asked me to write two letters. One to Roy, my uncle, and one as if Roy answered my letter.

LETTER TO ROY

Roy,

I've never called you uncle. You were always Roy to me.

It was a hot, summer day and I was visiting my aunt, your sister. I cannot recall whether my parents were visiting my aunt too, I only know that my brother was there.

You asked me to go upstairs with you to play and to "wrestle" a little bit. I remember that I was reluctant to go with you, as if I already knew what your intentions were.

Going upstairs to one of the bedrooms, you closed the curtains and urged me to come to bed to lay beside you.

I can still feel, taste how you touched me with your hands and your lips and how and where you made me touch you.

This was the first time that it happened and is still the strongest recollection of many of these events; one or many it feels like a blur or a dark place to go.

From that day on, I have this strong feeling of guilt, the feeling that I've done something so wrong that I felt ashamed thinking about it and even more ashamed to talk about it to anyone, including my parents, for many years. In fact, I've never told my parents.

You actually gave me five Dutch guilders (a lot of money for a seven-year-old, forty years ago) if I promised to keep it "our" secret.

What was driving you? Did you have no clue how wrong this was? Even as a boy, I knew this instinctively.

I felt dirty from that moment on. I developed an unusual interest in sex, maybe even an obsession. What bugs me the most is that you put a trigger deep down inside me, a trigger that when pulled could make me feel angry or intensely sad at unexpected times. Seeing a television show, hearing or reading a story could do the trick. It's always there, and I never know when it might hit me. But when it does, I cry and break down.

It was only when I met my current wife that I also found that you hurt something in me on an even deeper level. I sometimes hate it when she touches me or does something when we are intimate. It's not always the same. Oh, no, that would be too fair. It always surprises me, and it surprises my wife. If it happens, I push her away and want to be left alone. I sometimes yell at her that I don't need anyone. So, you didn't only affect my life, but also hers . . .

Through reading, I learned that people who have been abused are more likely to abuse others. I am still afraid that you've created a hidden monster in me--evil that comes out when I least expect it.

With all this, you've changed the trust I have in people and although I try to live with trusting others, I don't trust anyone around my kids or maybe I still don't trust anyone around me . . .

Deep down, I still believe that I am on my own, that I have to do everything by myself.

I am angry for what you've done to me. I am angry because I didn't stop you from doing this to others.

I am sad that I can't talk to my parents about my deepest secret.

I am not going to blame you for who I am or what I do today, that would be too much credit for you.

I forgave you after I learned that hatred doesn't bring me anything. But I still ask myself how you could brand a little kid for the rest of his life, for just a few moments of your own filthy need of pleasure.

Jean

LETTER TO JEAN

Jean,

I am talking to you from the other side of life. I have no excuses for what I've done and mostly it was like an external force took over to make me do the things I did.

This now sounds like a lame excuse, and I know it was wrong but couldn't stop it. I should have found help for my problem, but I didn't. There has never been a moment that I actually thought about the consequences of my actions, the outcomes for my victims. I know how wrong it was but again never contemplated not even for a moment what the long-term impact was of my deeds for a young kid like you.

If I were a sane person, I would have probably stopped conducting these activities, but I let my urges be the leader of my actions, fully selfish without any responsibilities. The only fear I had was that I would be caught, but even knowing what the repercussions could be didn't made me stop.

Mostly I was playing on the guilt feeling of my playmates. No one blew the horn, so I could safely go on doing what I was doing. I have no remorse of anything I did, while at the same time I didn't want anything bad to happen to you.

I did not deserve your forgiveness but knowing that you do forgive me makes me feel guilty after all.

Roy

CHAPTER 5

MY CHOICE ABOUT HOW TO REACT

As said in the introduction, this book is not meant to be a scientific analysis of sexual abuse and domestic violence survival. My story won't represent all survivors, but it offers my perspective. Over the years, I've noticed two important things. First, it's helpful for victims to hear the stories of other survivors. Second, there are undeniable commonalities between how I dealt with (and still deal with) day-to-day life issues and how I've seen other survivors dealing with their issues.

Although I sometimes wonder how my life would be if I weren't a victim, this is something I will never find out. So, I can never fully claim that my behavior and habits are all influenced by the events that happened in my youth.

I used to say that what happened to me in the past can never be an excuse of how I will act and behave today and in the future.

This probably would make a good quote, but I came to the insight that this claim is not entirely true. Our past has shaped us, whether we like it or not. How we deal with our past should be each and everyone's choice, but the impact of sexual abuse and domestic violence on me has been so big that I can only conclude (at least for me) that it has influenced and probably still influences the way I have been shaped and the shape of my life in the years to come.

LIFE IS SIMPLY HAPPENING

Life can throw you a few curveballs; that's part of life. But what if you had the feeling that life was only about dodging or catching curveballs? In other words, you just accept that unexpected things can and will happen all the time. Events occur that could turn something positive into something dark and negative. You would, besides a deep, unsafe feeling, also develop a sense that life is simply happening to you and perhaps that is the same thing.

I know this is not a book that tells about a happy boy growing up in a happy family, but that doesn't mean that there were no happy moments and occasions. Maybe in the end, there were way more happy moments than unhappy and scary moments. The point is that the bad moments were really bad, and they happened always when I least expected. So, no matter how much fun we had at times, there was always this dark cloud glooming over us that things could go wrong in a heartbeat, in the blink of an eye, sometimes without any warning.

Either my siblings would start a fight, or my dad flipped his mood. This gave me the sense that life happens to me. Instead of being in charge of my life, I had to learn how to react and anticipate. We all, especially my sister and me, developed a sense, like a sort of a radar, that could track potential conflicts, which we often tried to defuse, but so often we either missed them or failed.

The good thing is, I became good at handling conflicts (perhaps all bad things have a good side after all). On the other hand, it took me a while to get better in making choices more strategically. I learned to think on my feet and shoot from the hip but mastered less how to make choices with a positive, long-term result. Yes, I'm good at picking up the pieces, coming to the rescue, and responding, but that behavior is also reactive. I do think that this impulsive behavior, which was apparent in our family, had a deep influence on how I lived my life. I've also seen it in the lives of some of my siblings, too.

Being spontaneous is a good thing. Being impulsive can be dangerous and disastrous in anyone's life.

HANKERING FOR REAL LOVE

My whole life I've struggled about finding real love. There has always been this feeling in me that true love had to exist, not a relationship that will end up ugly, but a partnership that stays beautiful and romantic. Now call me a romantic, but is it so bad to strive for that? An everlasting love . . . sounds more like a Hollywood movie or the lyrics of a good love song. The thing is, I think something goes wrong in a child's mind when he or she is abused, beaten up, and yelled at, often by the same people who also give care, feed, and provide for the child. You don't need to be a psychologist or read all the research on the topic to know that this will distort the victim's view of what love is or how love should be.

Instinctively, we know what love is and I guess so did I. I loved the loved and still love the parents, for which I so often was afraid of too. I should love my uncle, after all he was family and he was sometimes nice. But why did those people hurt me time after time? How should I, and can I, love them back?

In response, I can see how other victims would have used violence. This is, however, not how I dealt with my situation. Although I must say I often felt a deep anger and wanted to break stuff at times; there were instances when I did. What I broke more were not physical things; they were emotional things.

I had a hard time keeping a relationship healthy. I didn't learn how to solve problems effectively. When in a conflict, I either would shut down or use too much verbal strength—not yelling but breaking someone into submission with logic and reason. It was so important for me to win every argument and discussion, with little respect for the other person. I hated myself for doing this, but I couldn't stop it. I've improved greatly, but I am still working on it.

Mood Swings

I always thought that my mood swings were a "family trait," as my dad had mood swings, and most of my siblings had mood swings. What I didn't see is that mood swings are not a character trait, but they are a result of something else. Little did I know that there was a correlation between our behaviors, our moods, and the explosive situations we often lived in. I dare to say that these crazy mood swings in all of us created many of the explosive situations in the family.

My dad could go from a real good mood to something really bad in a moment. He also had days when he was hardly approachable, just because he was grumpy. Not only did I start to see that being grumpy and having bad mood swings is a selfish act, I also understand now why we had so many fights in the family. It was like we were always agitated, and things could go wrong really fast when we had an argument. As a kid, this only added to the lack of safety I already felt, and I'm sure many of my siblings had those feelings too.

Coming back to the correlation, we all grew up in an abusive and violent family. My dad had the same upbringing and was an alcoholic too. His war trauma didn't do anything positive for his moods. All in all, I think I see the reasons why most of us in the family had unstable mental states. But the fact remains—because of all this, I personally felt unsafe at home, the place where a kid should feel the safest.

I wish I could tell you that these mood swings were over for me when I left my parents' home. But that was not the case. It took me years, until I got the insight that having bad moods is not a choice, but giving in to the dark mood and letting it affect your surroundings is a choice.

TRUST ISSUES

As I mentioned previously, I developed a strong feeling that no person could be fully trusted. I always had walls around me and I became a master of masking them. While I tried to fit in the "normal" world by doing normal stuff and following the rules, I also searched for love, understanding, and being accepted. That's still a process that I'm working on today.

FINDING PASSION

This book is also about what I did when I discovered that my life was not driven by my passion. In the end, it's perhaps not even so important how I came to that point. You are blessed if you already live your passion and fulfill your life's purpose. But if you don't, then I hope this book will help inspire you to pursue a passion-driven life.

My life now is good. After twenty-five years working for the corporate world, it was time to pursue a different path. A path of my passion for dance and what is close to my heart, the fight against sexual abuse and the empowerment of women.

Why things in our lives happen and go the way they did go is certainly not an easy question to answer, if it can be answered at all. This question also goes a little beyond the intentions of this book. What I would like to say about it is that bad things can happen to us all, and whether the cause of these events are due to our choices is another hard and difficult topic. What is easier to understand is that the reaction to what happened to us is more in our peripheral of what we can decide. In other words, *we don't always have a choice of the circumstances we get into, but we do have a choice how we react to our circumstances.*

Now one-liners like these always sounds so good on Facebook or on a little tile we can put on the wall, but can we make them work and apply them in life? When I got abused as young as I was, I don't think I had a lot of conscious ability to make good choices. Later in life, I think I made better choices.

We never know for sure how much influence our past experiences have on our current and future behaviors. Would I have been a better or different person had I not been abused? I'll never find an answer to that question. What I do know is that I became a fighter, a survivor with persistence and tenacity, because of these events. I believe that I've been blessed with a strong will to turn all this bad into something else.

I truly feel that we need to live life on our own terms. Not selfishly, but in service of others. The more I studied life, which I felt compelled to do to make sense out of all that has occurred in my own life, the more I learned to set aside the things I see happening in the world. There is still so much injustice in the world—the wars, the hunger, the gaps between rich and poor. We see this on a global scale but also on a much smaller scale all around us.

I always believed that life should be led from our core and our passion. What I also learned is that a lot of things that happen to us will keep us outside of living from our passion and our core.

If I fast-forward in time, I can say that I live in Dallas, Texas, with my partner. She and I have been together for more than seven years now. We met at work. She still works where we met, but I bid the corporate world goodbye after more than twenty-five years to pursue my passions of coaching dancers, empowering women, and fighting the fight against sexual abuse. I founded my own company and developed my coaching model, "The Dorff Inner-Strength Method." I have customers from around the globe whom I serve. I often travel to Europe to be closer to my children and other family. I can say that I used my bad experiences to fuel a passionately driven life. This almost sounds like the end of the book and my story, but I'd like to tell you how I came to this thriving point in my life.

CHAPTER 6

LIVING FROM YOUR CORE

For a long time, I lived a life primarily to stay within boundaries set by others, trying to meet other people's expectations and not my own goals. Living a pragmatic life, I was afraid to make mistakes or to bend the rules too much. I expressed my passion only surface deep, more in the hobby sphere and to create an image than to use it as a leading force and integral part of my life.

I discovered a passion for dance, Latin American ballroom dancing. It is the dynamics of movement, the interaction between a man and a woman, the emotions and use of energy, and the music that attracts me. It is the aspects of theatre, art, and competition. It's all about creation that gives joy and allows self-expression. All aspects of life can be seen and expressed in one dance and sometimes in one single movement.

I love dance as a spectator, as a teacher, but more so as a dancer. On the dance floor, I feel at home. It's hard to describe my passion for dance. It feels like I can keep on writing about it, while at the same time no words can actually express my passion for dance accurately enough. Perhaps this is a proof that passion needs to be lived.

To live a life driven by passion, we also need to have a good understanding of our core nature, our personality type, our basic motivations in life, our core talents, and preferences.

Like other people with a past of child abuse, I was not true to my core nature, perhaps even in conflict with it. I was more pragmatic and analytic than being intuitive and empathic, as my natural inclination is. I tried to be a conformist against my more creative and explorative nature.

I believe it is impossible and unnatural to hide our true nature completely. I, for instance, was always looking for change and could never be truly content with where I was, what I had, and ultimately who I was. I carried this for a long time as a secret in me. The result was that I was restless and always searching for something, not exactly knowing what.

In hindsight, I can see that this was not easy for my partner and often unsettling for her. This all doesn't mean that I had a completely unhappy life or that it was all negative. But I had to hit a really low point in life to realize this. Hopefully we don't all have to go through something tough to see that we should follow our passion and fulfill our life's purpose. But let's set our life stories aside for a moment. The question we need to ask ourselves is: "How would life be if my core nature and passion were aligned and worked together?"

We can't redo the past, but we can change the way we look at the past. By accepting that learning is everything, failures cease to exist. And so, it was that I accepted my experiences as tools and building blocks for the future. It was now up to me how and if to use them. With dancing as my passion, and a better understanding of my core nature, it was time to initiate action and find out if this would take me closer to my life's purpose.

My story would not be complete if I don't tell you about my faith. I was also a searcher in this area. Always a believer in a higher power but not willing to commit to any specific religion until the Lord started to talk to me in my mid-forties. I am probably a hard learner because when he communicated at that time, he had already talked to me about dancing as part of my life's purpose. I understand now that I had to start walking and take action to grasp how the Lord meant his words, instead of passively waiting for more clues as I did for almost another five years.

For me, Christian faith means that I let myself be guided by him and that I conform myself to his will and accept his grace. The skeptical reader might say that I swapped from conforming to other people's expectations to conforming to something vague, like faith, and that I didn't make such a drastic change after all. Maybe so, but for me accepting Christ and his grace filled a void in me that I thought could never be filled completely. And to start walking a new path driven by my passion could never be done if I didn't let it be guided by faith.

One thing I've learned throughout my life is that many people in life walk through a fog, a mist of thoughts, concerns, and worries. Once in a while the fog disappears and makes room for periods of brightness. Those are the times that we feel happy and creative, times when it seems that our senses work better and are more sensitive. Most of us accept this coming and going as something natural, something that we can only influence to some extent. I was no different.

But nothing is more beside the truth than this. We can choose to have "no fog" or at least less fog in our lives. We can choose to live from our core, where we feel gratitude for life, and we can choose to use our ordeals not as stones that wear us down, but as stepping stones to go farther in life.

When something traumatic happens to our lives, in my case sexual abuse, we often thicken the fog we are already in. We sometimes say that there is a light at the end of the tunnel. Seeing life that way makes us go forward because we think we can actually see that light at the end of the tunnel. But as we move forward, it feels that the light isn't getting any closer. It feels like the light is an illusion, unreachable. But the thing is, *the light at the end of the tunnel is not the illusion, the tunnel you walk in is the illusion.* It is self-created through your mind, self-created through worries, frustration, and fears. If we dissolve the tunnel, at least the majority part, you will see that light is all around us. Not living from your core, not following your passion: that is what is creating that tunnel through which we only see a light far in the distance.

You might wonder what the tunnel is. The tunnel is often a stacking of false beliefs and fears layer upon layer. Once we can see our false beliefs and dissolve our fears or know how to do things despite our fears, we'll start living from our core. Being blocked by false beliefs and fears is almost always a mental and physical state.

CHAPTER 7

THE FIVE ENERGIES

This chapter is meant to give you a good introduction to the Dorff Inner-Strength Method and the model of five energies. The illustrations are intended to give you more insight into where you are within each of these energies. None of the energies is more important the other; they are not just interrelated, they are one energy. The Dorff Inner-Strength Method helps you to see and to feel that, but most importantly, to support you further on your growth path to find a thriving life of passion and compassion.

Where does the Dorff Inner-Strength Method come from? Why do I believe it works so well? After years of experience as a business manager, an athlete, a coach, and a teacher, I started to need a modality to support and coach people better. I wanted that modality to be usable, no matter in what phase of personal development someone is. This modality should always give a clear understanding of where someone is and what could and should be improved to live a more thriving and passionate life.

I'd like to tell you that I spent years and years developing this model, and maybe I did subconsciously. I have to admit that one night a few years ago, I had the inspiration (I like to call it inspiration from God) to draw and write this model the way it is presented here. The Dorff Inner-Strength Method is a holistic model. I describe it here in different parts, but it has to be seen as a whole, where each part is equally important, and none can be left out.

A Model for All

By far, most sexual abusers are men. In almost all cases, it's a family member or a close friend. So then, why not a program that educates men? Because I also believe that we need to raise awareness more broadly, including men and women.

Everyone should know these important concepts.

- Recognize the abuser.
- Recognize the victim.
- Change our attitudes.
- Defend ourselves.
- Get out of the victim loop.
- Start thriving again.

There is power in making women aware that they do have the power to say this is not how my story is going to end. Hearing it from a survivor and a man gives this a different perspective.

The Dorff Inner-Strength Method, therefore, is a coaching program that helps and supports everyone (not only abuse and domestic violence victims) who needs to find a life of passion and purpose; who needs to not just get by but thrive in all aspects of life. It's a holistic method where all the described energies: physical energy, mental energy, creative energy, manifestation energy, and divine energy will be connected and brought back into balance. This ultimately leads to a richer life for those who have gone through this program.

The Dorff Inner-Strength Method works on the body and the mind and lets you create the life you want on your terms. After the "thrive to survive" program, you will be able to say the following:

- I am comfortable in my body.
- I am confident and take on new challenges.
- I have trust in myself and others.
- I build strong, new relationships.
- I am personally and professionally successful.

Everything is energy. I am certainly not the first to write about it and certainly not the first to talk about it. Everything is energy, even if you would exactly grasp what that means, then why is that relevant for you as a person? Why would it be important to understand if you, for instance, want to change your life or just leave a life, in general?

The Dorff Inner-Strength model won't give the answers to these questions. But it will help you to look differently at yourself with the purpose to understand yourself better, to understand what drives you, and perhaps why things don't go the way you might want. In the end, everything is energy, one energy: The divine energy.

I've described it as five energies, but I am a strong believer that everything comes from one source, from one energy. I was inspired by that one source—I call it God (and leave it up to you what you call it)—to write and further develop this model.

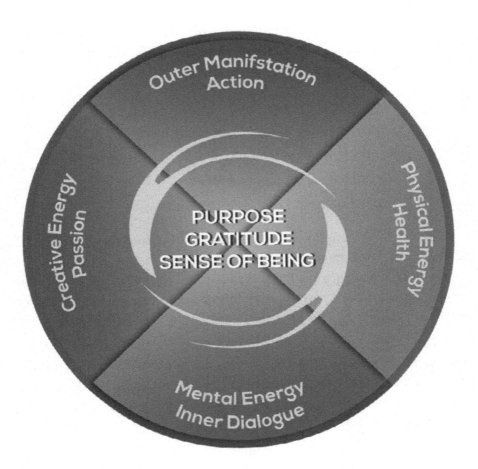

The model of Five Energies: One energy expressed in five ways

1. PHYSICAL ENERGY

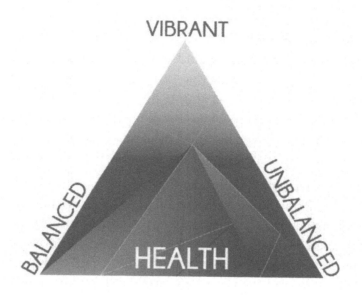

Physical Energy: Expressed by how vibrant your body is

Because abuse victims are often so young when they were robbed of their innocence and happiness, they have a hard time to live to the fullest and to believe that true happiness truly exists. The fear of happiness is real for them, because victims often believe that happiness is unreal and not something for them. How strange this might seem, but sexual abuse and domestic violence victims often sabotage their own chances for happiness.

Most victims have lost their feelings of safety and trust, lost the confidence to say something about how to run their own lives, because they were violated mentally and physically in their private space in the most intimate way. I was violently penetrated physically by my uncle against my own will. Whether it was a one-time act or multiple times, like in my case, the impact of these acts on the future life of victims is obviously big but still not fully understood.

The violent invasion of my body as a young kid often made me feel that my body was not fully my own any more. So often when something happened to me, my body would just shut down. After the abuse started, I developed the feeling that I needed a lot of physical attention, while at the same time it was almost impossible to fully accept it. So often I got hugely triggered when things became too intimate. I love to give myself over to a lover, but then, at some point, this huge fear came up that I either would be hurt, or memories of the rapes came up.

Despite what happened to me, I do think I was also blessed. From a young age, I started to learn how to use my body advantageously, first as a martial artist and later also as a dancer. In both disciplines, I was fortunate to reach high levels. Through this, I developed a deep understanding of how the human body works, and I soon discovered that the stronger and the more comfortable I felt in my own body, the easier it was for me to cope with other things in my life, including my sexual-abuse past. In other words, the more vibrant my body was, the better it was and is for me.

How Dancing Worked for Me

Due to the abuses, I got really disconnected from my body; I lost the sense of seeing the body and the mind as two parts of a whole. It's maybe not a disconnect from just the body and mind, per se, because they can work well together while still being out of balance and disconnected. Rather, it's a disconnect between body and mind on the one side and the soul on the other that causes a great unbalance.

I was so young that I didn't notice immediately that there was something wrong—a disconnect. In my case, I was well trained as a martial artist and a dancer. But something was missing. Martial arts worked well, or at least I thought it did, as I learned how to channel and block my emotions. This skill was already there due to the only survival mechanism I knew: I knew how to block my emotions to not feel any pain and to be able to step away from memories.

This skill is purely a survival tactic. In my adult life, I felt that I could not live my life to the fullest, although I didn't know how to articulate that. How could I? Can you describe something you have not experienced or have only limited experience of? Can you describe a taste you have never tasted?

In hindsight, one of the greater components that I missed throughout my life is a full spectrum of how to express myself emotionally. Not knowing that I grew up in family where we basically all suffered from this, I was unaware of this until I branched out in life. Then I really came to see this omission when I started to study dance and how to express emotions through movement.

If I look at the life of my siblings, at least some of them, then only from this point things become much clearer why they behaved in certain ways. There was a limited scale of emotional expression, primitive almost. There was happiness or anger, with little between. It's really hard to recognize this poor ability of expressing emotions when you are excluded from a richer way of experiencing and expressing them. Most of my siblings started to look for deeper experiences later in life, either through art forms, such as dancing, painting, and other creative expression.

When I started to study dance, I started to understand that we should not only express life as happiness, but more so that we should be able to express the full range of emotions to reflect life more realistically. It was also then that I really felt that I was better able to express emotions through dance, but I still limited myself in real life.

I saw that dance can be a reflection of life. *It was then that I saw that dance could be a conduit for learning and expressing emotions.* My goal in dance is to become transparent and show that it's not only the dancer who experiences more emotions but also the spectator who is invited to experience a deeper and wider range of emotions by watching the dancers expressing theirs.

I challenged myself to use dance, hence my body and mind, to express and experience more. Without really looking for it, I unlocked something in me that had been lingering there, perhaps waiting to be unlocked. Something that was never lost, it was just never unlocked. Soon after this, I discovered that when I move with people, I can feel their emotional life. By connecting, I can offer them to experience more and to express more.

A connected body, mind, and soul heals by accepting circumstances and not blocking them or hiding. *The path **from** something is only found in the path **to** something.*

I have a strong need to connect movement with both healing from sexual abuse and female empowerment. That movement is not necessarily dance—that is just a really nice way of moving for me. *It is finding freedom in the body again that helps finding freedom in the mind and a more connected soul.* I came to believe that this is especially true for those whose bodies have been violated by abuse.

We live in a disconnected world, where a connected body and mind is not necessary anymore. We only have to look around us to see that this is true. Many people cannot, or find it difficult to, move comfortably and with ease. We come up with all kinds of phenomena and even illness to explain why this is so.

One big cause of this is the lack of exercise. Our work habits, compared to the generations of years past, have changed dramatically. Most people work from behind a desk, staring at an electronic device, like the one I'm writing this book on now. Our transportation is primarily done by vehicles that remove any physical effort on our part. All of this means that to "move" has become a choice; exercise is optional. This causes so many physical problems.

It's obvious to see a connection between the way we live our lives and the way our bodies developed and the way we move. You can only imagine that when our bodies (and minds) are violated at a young age, this phenomenon of the disconnected body only gets worse. Knowing what happened to me, but not fully understanding what that had done to me, I had to find respect for my body, not only for my body, but also for other people's bodies.

Not respecting your body can take many forms; self-mutilation is one of the most extreme. I didn't go quite as far as that, but in hindsight I can see that I was weirdly obsessed with my own body and other people's bodies, mostly sexual driven. In short, I started to feel that I had to find respect for my body and learn how to honor my body again in a healthy way.

It's good when we are healthy and can use our body well, as it restores and maintains balance. The saying, "a healthy mind in a healthy body" (Latin: *mens sana in corpore sano*), although a little out of context here, is utterly true. A healthy body should be seen here as having trust in and respect for your body and the bodies of others.

Now, does that mean that you cannot have a healthy mind when your body isn't healthy? This goes a little beyond this book, but I can at least offer an opinion. I do think that people can have a healthy mind in a less-healthy body, but they should always strive for the optimum.

2. MENTAL ENERGY

Mental Energy: Expressed by your inner dialogue

A balanced mind can easily be measured by following your self-talk. Ask yourself, "How do I talk to myself?" Is it encouraging and positive or is it denigrating and negative? One of the signs of a balanced mind is if can you sit in silence without the need to fill your mind with thoughts all the time. Negatively wired minds have a harder time to sit in silence than positive minds.

It's hard to say if my self-talk would have developed differently if I hadn't been abused. What I do know is that many times it was really hard to silence my self-talk and to push it in a more positive direction. What always helped me was prayer and meditation. At first, I just prayed and meditated the way I thought I should do it, only later did I read and learn about how to pray and meditate.

In general, I think learning these two things helped me. I was able to stay more in balance than I have seen from other abuse victims who were less aware of the influence of their inner dialogue on their overall wellbeing.

I wish I could tell you that the impact of my sexual abuse was only physically felt. Unfortunately, I think that the mental impact of abuse is greater than the physical impact. It's, however, more difficult to see that.

The emotional expression I mentioned before is obviously as much a mental process as a physical process. The mental side for me is that looking at the emotions in the context of dance was creating a safe place to explore and to experience. It was not that I started to dance to address this. I discovered it while studying dance. What felt natural to me was to see the connection between healing from a trauma and moving the body.

But more than anything, I changed the way I thought about things. You have to be able to express yourself freely, both physically and mentally. The caveat here is that if you go into this process by yourself, you don't know what "freely" is.

This is how I can best describe it. If you were born in prison, how would you know what freedom is? It's like an animal born in captivity. Is it domesticated or just hugely constricted in its natural freedom and abilities?

Can you know what your capacity and abilities are if they've never been explored or experienced? As humans, we all are receptive for building and creating false beliefs. Sexual abuse victims typically have a few more. These beliefs have limited me too. But I always knew something was off. My authenticity was violated, although I had no clue what that meant. In the moments of freedom, I did not know what do with it.

Moments of gluttony were often there. In my case, it was not so much in food, but definitely in physical indulgences with sex. I always had to try things in excess, if I started to read, I read for hours and hours. All new things I consumed excessively, like I didn't know how to put a limit on things.

Now, with a balanced mind, things have come together in better balance.

3. Creative Energy

Creative Energy: Expressed by how passionately you lead your life

Yes, I felt the passion energy in me but hardly knew how to combine that with my physical and mental energy. Hence my imagination became limited. So, for a long time, I was a conformist doing only things that could withstand the judgment of others. This is by itself a limited behavior. I think that it was not so much the sexual abuse that caused this but the domestic violence my siblings and I lived under. Whereas some of my siblings became utterly rebellious and went against my father's authority, I was either openly or secretly always looking for his approval, or later for approval from authority figures in my life in general.

So, was I a passionate person? I like to believe so, but that is different from living a passionate life. Or better yet to use your passion to create a more positive life. Being hotheaded is definitely passionate but not necessarily positive.

When I found dancing, I found my passion, but at first more than anything else, I was still looking for approval from others. I cannot say that I was fully aware of this, but it is definitely clear for me in hindsight. It's only in the past ten years or so that I have dared to explore and follow my instincts and intuition in my teaching and dancing.

The word freedom arises again here. The influence of abuse and domestic violence is that it really limits a victim in the way he or she experiences life and ultimately expresses himself or herself in life. An abuse victim is robbed of so much. Creative energy is the source for everyone to create a life of abundance and happiness. For creativity, you need to have a sense of freedom, a sense of fearlessness. It's hard to talk in generalizations, so I can only express my own experiences.

Through dance, I discovered that I was not the analytical and pragmatic person I was led to believe I was. Being analytical and pragmatic was just another coping mechanism to deal with the world the way I saw it and the way the world treated me, at least in my young, formative years. By accessing my more creative and empathic nature, I was led to dancing and to healing. I'm an extrovert, and the need to express myself overtook me. Ultimately, that led me to start my coaching business and write this book.

4. MANIFESTATION ENERGY

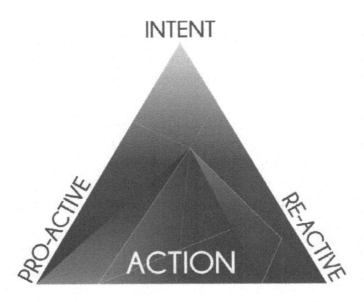

Manifestation Energy: Expressed by what you produce in life

By being limited by the first three energies (physical, mental, and creative energies), what I produced in life was limited too. Sure, I had successes in relationships, sports, and business. But they always came with a cost. There was seldom a good balance. There was always a big sense of self-obsession.

In the process, I probably have hurt people around me, especially those I loved the most. Now, I don't want to use my abuse as an excuse for my wrongdoings and neither should you. But, unfortunately, we cannot escape the fact that abuse has a deep impact on how people live their lives long after the abuse.

It's not only the physical pain and the mental torment at the time of the abuse that are only tragedies. The saddest thing is the long-term impact it has on a person's life. Most abuse victims cannot live life to the fullest. They often settle for just getting by. Heck, it took me years to see that just surviving was not enough; life is for thriving and not just surviving.

In the end, it is all about what we produce in our lives. What are the fruits we offer? There is a strong relation between how you run your internal energies (physical, mental, and creative) and the fruits you produce and give.

Abuse victims, like me, have a large internal world. It's a world that seems hard to escape. Even when it looks good on the outside, the battles fought inside never stop. On the other hand, when we have the will to produce good things in life, to manifest a life of abundance, freedom, and happiness, it drives us to heal and improve our lives in relation to all the five energies.

There is a way out! Starting to produce more positive things in life will also increase your energies in the other areas and vice versa. Opt for the first three energies, and you will produce better and more positive things in life.

5. DIVINE ENERGY

Divine Energy or Sense of Being: Expressed by purpose and gratitude

Why should I believe in God after all that's happened?

There is a sense of being—the feeling that there is more in life than what we see, that somehow everything is related and connected. This doesn't mean you necessarily need to believe in a god or a higher power. In my case, I do. As I've done in this whole book, I can give you only my perspective. Because you are still with me, I assume you are still interested in what I have to say.

I can easily see that people would actually lose faith in a divine figure after a life of abuse and domestic violence. In my case, it's almost the opposite. What happened in my life actually brought me to God.

I previously shared about how I was able to forgive my uncle. With the forgiveness, other things became clearer to me too. We cannot always create new beginnings, no matter how much we sometimes want to, but we can certainly create different endings.

Before the forgiveness, I tried to fight the darkness in my heart with more darkness. Anger, hate, and fear are all forms of darkness that either keep our lives small or even destroy them completely. I found that there is only one way to drive out the darkness— not with darkness, but with light.

As the late Dr. Martin Luther King Jr. said, "Hate cannot drive out hate; only love can do that." It's a more encompassing love than the love we naturally have for our family, partner, and perhaps close friends. It's finding love for life itself; it's finding love in the creations around us. It's the feeling that you are part of something bigger than yourself. It's the feeling that we can all be great, because there is always someone we can serve. I call this a "sense of being" or the "divine energy."

For more information about the Dorff Inner-Strength Method and the model of five energies, please visit **http://www.jeandorff.com**

CHAPTER 8

STEPPING INTO
THE WORLD

I might not live to see the glory, but I will continue the fight. The fight against domestic violence and sexual abuse.

Now that this book is finished, you might ask, "What is next?" My goal is simple. I want to reduce the number of sexual abuse cases dramatically—ideally stopping them completely. A big dream!

We need to drive out abuse as we would a common disease. We need to care about this as much as we care about bringing the numbers down for cancer, heart disease, and so on. We need to address this together as a community that is serious about creating a healthy and safe society for all its members, especially those who are most vulnerable. Reducing the number of sexual abuse cases can only be done if we have solidarity on this issue.

The publishing of this book has been made possible by the donations of many people, for which I am forever grateful. However, going through the process of raising funds, I had to strike up conversations with many people in person and by email. The one thing that struck me while having these conversations was that so many people find it really hard to even react when reading or hearing a story like mine, just because of the shock of it. People really don't know what they can do about abuse and domestic violence, other than perhaps donating money. For this reason, I have founded a nonprofit organization: A Dancer's Movement to Stop Sexual Abuse. This organization has the mission to develop and implement concrete programs and initiatives to raise awareness for and strive to stop sexual abuse. You'll find more information about this at the end of this chapter.

I hope my story will give people the courage to tell their story too. Because that's where it all has to start. We have to start with "breaking the silence." We have to give sexual abuse a face. In my book, I talk about numbers—hundreds of thousands of victims per year. That's more than 1,000 per day. It's one per minute. But it's not a number, it's a person. It's not a case, it's a person. It's a person with a name, with a family, with a life.

- Eveline from Texas, eighteen years old

one minute later …

- Hilde from Germany, six years old

one minute later …

- Gertrude from Arkansas, twelve years old

one minute later …

- Trudy from New York, seventeen years old

one minute later …

- Kimberly from California, fifty-three years old

one minute later …

- John from Minnesota, five years old

and the clock keeps ticking.

Sexual abuse victims are not nameless. We are not numbers in a report; we are people tainted for the rest of our lives. My name is Jean Dorff, abused from the age of seven. It's so normal to say you had cancer and you're fighting it, or you survived. However, to say that you were a sexual abuse victim is something else.

So, my next steps are these.

1. Go beyond just raising awareness for sexual abuse by starting a movement against sexual abuse: **A Dancer's Movement to Stop Sexual Abuse.**

2. Give victims the courage to step forward and break the silence. **I tell my story so there is one less story to tell.**

3. Empower women, who are more likely to be victims of sexual abuse and domestic violence than men. **We all have the power to say: This is not how my story is going to end.**

There is one goal: Reduce the number of abuse victims!

So, what can you do?

- If you are a victim, tell your story!

- Connect me with anyone or any organization that could help me fight this battle!

- Give a copy of this book to someone you think would be served by it! A part of the proceeds of my book go directly to the nonprofit organization, A Dancer's Movement to Stop Sexual Abuse.

Go to www.1less2tell.org and write your story. If you truly want to help make a difference, tell your story. Help to give sexual abuse a face. You can do it anonymously. I would be grateful for your openness.

Let me also tell you more about the nonprofit organization, A Dancer's Movement to Stop Sexual Abuse.

The purpose of **A Dancer's Movement to Stop Sexual Abuse** is primarily, but not exclusively, to reach out to dancers around the world, to create a united front, and to raise awareness for sexual abuse.

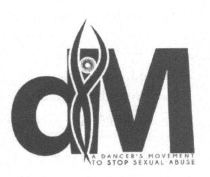

There are three focus areas.

1. *Support and coach* victims to overcome the trauma of sexual abuse and help them to lead a thriving life instead of just surviving. We have coaching programs based on the five energies (discussed previously) that will help victims and their close acquaintances power through these experiences into a transformed life.

2. *Raising awareness* in society by speaking events, social media outreach, and building a community of dancers and people who care for this cause, either within or outside the nonprofit. The first step is to encourage conversations about this issue, by asking victims to tell their story, so there is one less story to tell.

3. *Educate and empower* women, men, especially young adults. A Dancer's Movement to Stop Sexual Abuse has developed specific workshops and trainings to educate people about this topic. We have effective training sessions for corporate organizations about how to deal with and prevent sexual harassment in the workplace. We also provide self-defense classes specifically focused on women's strengths and capabilities, informing them about potentially dangerous scenarios, and how to react in these situations. The goal with these workshops is to create a more prepared and better educated world, where people voice their

concerns and are empowered to react with preventative actions. We have been asked to develop a specific training program for high school graduates, the teaching staff, and parents.

For each focus area of A Dancer's Movement to Stop Sexual Abuse we have and will develop specific programs. A Dancer's Movement to Stop Sexual Abuse will raise funding not only to support its own programs and initiatives but to also support other programs and initiatives. Visit www.adancersmovement.org for more information.

You can also follow A Dancer's Movement to Stop Sexual Abuse on Facebook: https://www.facebook.com/adancersmovement

I thank you for reading my book. Perhaps you bought it, perhaps someone gave it you. In any case, it might not be appropriate to say, "I hope you enjoyed it." What I do hope is that it gives you courage if you are a victim, that it gives you understanding and awareness if you know a victim, or if you just feel sympathy for this cause.

By reading this book, you've already started to make a change, for which I'm forever grateful. If you want to leave me a reaction, go to my website www.jeandorff.com. You'll find a special page about this book.

With deep gratitude, I say, "Here is to your growth."

Jean Dorff

WHAT IS SEXUAL ABUSE?

The scars of sexual abuse are more often invisible than visible. A few minutes of unwanted fondling can have equally long-lasting damaging effects as can years of sexual abuse. It doesn't matter whether it was a single incident or multiple acts over a longer period of time. There is no good way to measure what story is more severe than another or what causes more harmful effects. Sexual abuse in any case cannot and should not be minimized. Anything that has been done to a person without their consent is abuse.

Any type of sexual experience you did not want to take part in is sexual abuse. Whether this was physical, verbal, or whether you were forced to look at something of a sexual nature, such as body parts or pornographic material. Even when you participated, even when it felt good, even when you got something for it, and even when you had pleasure from it, it can still be abuse. If you were a child when this happened, it definitely was abuse.

The bottom line is when someone with more leverage and power convinced, hustled, coerced, tricked, or forced any one with less power into any type of sexual experience, it is abuse. Does the abuser always have to be an older person? With child abuse, it is always the case. With adult abuse, that is not necessarily so, but regardless, whatever the age you were taken advantage of, it was sexual abuse.

Sexual abuse often goes together with physical violence, but if it didn't, it's still sexual abuse. One way for you to know whether you were abused is to answer the following questions.

1. Was the activity against your will? If yes, then it was abuse.
2. Were you too young (under the age of eighteen) to make a judgment of the activity? If yes, then it was abuse.

In other words, when it doesn't feel good, it isn't good; when you say no, it should mean no. (But even when we don't say no, it still can be abuse.) Victim's stories and allegations should always be taken seriously.

According to www.loveisrespect.org, sexual abuse can be defined like this.

> Sexual abuse refers to any action that pressures or coerces someone to do something sexually they don't want to do. It can also refer to behavior that impacts a person's ability to control their sexual activity or the circumstances in which sexual activity occurs, including oral sex, rape or restricting access to birth control and condoms.

Moreover, this site further states that it is important to know that just because the victim "didn't say no," doesn't mean that they meant "yes." When someone does not resist an unwanted sexual advance, it doesn't mean that they consented. Sometimes physically resisting can put a victim at a bigger risk for further physical or sexual abuse.

Statistics from the Rape, Abuse & Incest National Network (RAINN) webpage shows the rampant and desperate cry of sexual abuse cases. These are the number of people victimized each year.

- Inmates: 80,600 were sexually assaulted or raped.
- Children: 60,000 were victims of "substantiated or indicated" sexual abuse.
- General Public: 321,500 Americans 12 and older) were sexually assaulted or raped.
- Military: 18,900 experienced unwanted sexual contact.
- Every 98 seconds another American is sexually assaulted.

As many of you have experienced, children are not spared from the claws of sexual abuse: 15 percent of sexual assault and rape victims are under age twelve, while 29 percent are ages twelve to seventeen. The highest risk years are ages twelve to thirty-four. Girls between the ages of sixteen to nineteen are four times more likely to be victims of rape, attempted rape, or sexual assault.

The Central Minnesota Sexual Assault Center gives the following statistics.

- 7 percent of girls in grades 5-8 and 12 percent of girls in grades 9-12 said they had been sexually abused.
- 3 percent of boys grades 5-8 and 5 percent of boys in grades 9-12 said they had been sexually abused.

Combatting this issue has not been regarded as a top priority among law enforcement officers and politicians. It is more important that sexual abuse victims come forward and be strong enough at putting this evil activity to a halt. The victim's voice must once and for all be heard.

Sources

- www.loveisrespect.org
- www.rainn.org
- www.cmsac.org

APPENDIX B

WHAT IS DOMESTIC VIOLENCE?

Domestic violence is the willful intimidation, physical assault, battery, sexual abuse, and/or other abusive behavior as part of a systematic pattern of power and control perpetrated by one intimate partner against another. It includes physical violence, sexual violence, psychological violence, and emotional abuse. The frequency and severity of domestic violence can vary dramatically; however, the one constant component of domestic violence is one partner's consistent efforts to maintain power and control over the other.

Domestic violence is an epidemic affecting individuals in every community, regardless of age, economic status, sexual orientation, gender, race, religion, or nationality. It is often accompanied by emotionally abusive and controlling behavior that is only a fraction of a systematic pattern of dominance and control. Domestic violence can result in physical injury, psychological trauma, and, in severe cases, even death. The devastating physical, emotional, and psychological consequences of domestic violence can cross generations and last a lifetime.

For anonymous, confidential help, available 24/7, call the National Domestic Violence Hotline at 1-800-799-7233 (SAFE) or 1-800-787-3224 (TTY).

It is not always easy to determine in the early stages of a relationship if one person will become abusive. Domestic violence intensifies over time. Abusers might initially seem wonderful and perfect, but gradually become more aggressive and controlling as the relationship continues. Abuse might begin with behaviors that could easily be dismissed or downplayed, such as name calling, minor threats, possessiveness, or distrust.

Abusers might apologize profusely for their actions or try to convince the person they are abusing that they do these things out of love. However, violence and control always intensify over time with an abuser, despite the apologies. What might start out as something that was first believed to be harmless (for example, wanting the victim to spend all his or her time only with the abuser because the abuser loves the victim so much) escalates into extreme control and abuse (for example, threatening to kill or hurt the victim or others if he or she speaks to family, friends, etc.). Some examples of abusive tendencies (from the National Domestic Violence website) include, but are not limited, to the following.

- Tells you that you can never do anything right
- Shows extreme jealousy of your friends and time spent away
- Keeps you or discourages you from seeing friends or family members
- Insults, demeans or shames you with put-downs
- Controls every penny spent in the household
- Takes your money or refuses to give you money for necessary expenses
- Looks at you or acts in ways that scare you
- Controls who you see, where you go, or what you do
- Prevents you from making your own decisions

- Tells you that you are a bad parent or threatens to harm or take away your children
- Prevents you from working or attending school
- Destroys your property or threatens to hurt or kill your pets
- Intimidates you with guns, knives or other weapons
- Pressures you to have sex when you don't want to or do things sexually you're not comfortable with
- Pressures you to use drugs or alcohol

It is important to note that domestic violence does not always manifest as physical abuse. Emotional and psychological abuse can often be just as extreme as physical violence. Lack of physical violence does not mean the abuser is any less dangerous to the victim, nor does it mean the victim is any less trapped by the abuser.

Additionally, domestic violence does not always end when the victim escapes the abuser, tries to terminate the relationship, and/or seeks help. Often, it intensifies because the abuser feels a loss of control over the victim. Abusers frequently continue to stalk, harass, threaten, and try to control the victim after the victim escapes.

In fact, the victim is often in the most danger directly following the escape of the relationship when they seek help. According to a PubMed article, one-fifth of homicide victims with restraining orders are murdered within two days of obtaining the order; one-third are murdered within the first month.

Unfair blame is frequently put on the victim of abuse because of assumptions that victims choose to stay in abusive relationships. The truth is that bringing an end to abuse is not a matter of the victim choosing to leave; it is a matter of the victim being able to safely escape the abuser, the abuser choosing to stop the abuse, or others (for example, law enforcement, courts) holding the abuser accountable for the abuse that was inflicted.

SOURCES

- www.thehotline.org
- https://www.ncbi.nlm.nih.gov/pubmed/18523113

ABOUT THE AUTHOR

Jean Dorff was born in 's-Hertogenbosch, the Netherlands. He currently resides in Texas, *U.S.A. BROKEN SILENCE: Living with Passion and Purpose after Sexual Abuse, A Dancer's Story* is Jean's first book.

Jean has been a successful international martial arts competitor and ballroom dancer. He developed an interest in movement at an early age, exploring the concept of "conscious movement," a term he developed to describe a connection of rhythm and movement with mind, body, and soul.

As a business professional, with twenty-five years' experience in the corporate world, Jean has provided business coaching and consultancy in the fields of marketing, product management, and business strategy, primarily for Fortune-100 companies.

Through his work in both the business and dance industries, he began to see the similarity between training dancers and training corporate leaders and discovered that performance coaching could produce top competitors, regardless of the arena. By merging and blending his knowledge of both business and movement, he developed the idea of "conscious movement" into unique performance coaching program. This resulted in the DORFF INNER-STRENGTH METHOD FOR DANCE AND PERFORMANCE. He expanded this method further for EMPOWERMENT, LIFESTYLE, and WOMEN'S SELF-DEFENSE. Using the Dorff Inner-Strength Method, Jean has coached several Dutch national champions and internationally successful dancers, as well as business professionals and individuals around the globe.

Even more than his professional background, it was his personal ordeals that gave him the drive to empower people to overcome their negative experiences and live the life they want. Jean is a victim of sexual abuse and domestic violence himself. Jean pledged to fight the battle against sexual abuse and domestic violence and made it his personal mission to demonstrate how he became (as he calls it) "unbroken" and help others. "I'm unbroken; let me unbreak you" is his motto.

Jean likes to call himself a Transformational Coach. He founded his own performance and empowerment coaching company several years ago and recently a non-profit organization, A Dancer's Movement to Stop Sexual Abuse. www.adancersmovement.org

He lives now in Dallas, TX and consults, teaches dance, coaches, and lectures nationally and internationally. He is an active writer on social media and has two blogs: www.jeandorff.com and www.liveanempoweredlife.com.

CONNECT WITH ME

Website: www.jeandorff.com

Facebook: https://www.facebook.com/jean.dorff

Twitter: https://twitter.com/jeanbd

Instagram: https://www.instagram.com/jeandorff/

Acknowledgments

The writing of this book has been a journey. It stirred me (triggered me) to a great extent and brought me a few times to a point where I questioned if life itself was still worth living. But in the end, I truly believe that this book also brought me healing and closure.

I want to thank all my siblings—Frans, Reny and Folkert, Edwin and Frank, Edith and Ton, Herman and Joke, Jacqueline and Jaap—for their support and their love and for sharing our sadness, anger, and, of course, also our joy for life. I specially want to mention my sister, Edith, who was the first person I started to talk to about our abuse. She has always given me the strength, the courage, and the reason to write this book.

To Alexandra, who helped and challenged me to make my story authentic and personal. You took care of me in my darkest moments. I will never forget and will always love you for how you have believed in me.

To Mom and Dad, please forgive me that I told the story the way I did. This is by no means because I did not believe you didn't love me and my siblings. I've told my story to show how deep the scars of abuse can be in a family that is affected by it. I will always love you.

To Natasja, my best friend forever, for the countless hours we have talked, laughed, and cried. I love you dearly.

To Nelleke, the mother of my children, who has lived with me for so long listening to my stories but also dealing with the first signs of depression caused by the abuse. You have not always seen the best of me. You will always have a special place in my heart.

To Ruud, my dance teacher, my therapist. Your lessons and sessions have been instrumental. I am not sure if I would have made it without you . . . forever in my heart.

To Susan, my friend and fellow writer, I admire your courage, but I mostly admire your ability to forgive. You are a true source of inspiration.

To Pastor Dan, who was one of the first to read a full copy of this book. Dan is one of the bold pastors at Chase Oaks Church, where we try not to close our eyes to what's going on in our society and know that what happens outside our church most likely also happens inside our church. Where we also tackle issues head-on with respect and without judgment.

To Susan, my "other" therapist. Your approach in seeing my strength, my empathy, and my intuition encouraged me to believe in my gift and step into my power.

To Marcel, my best friend, for always being able to make me laugh and see things in perspective. I love you Maatje.

To Brad, Ed, Steven, Jack, Todd, and Dean my buddies from the Chase Oaks men's group. These men are all heroes in my life.

To Ben and all my fellow Shadow Light coaches, including Mark, Joe, and Vanessa. Our trainings have not only taught me how to help others, but they have helped empower me, too.

To Adam, Nicole, Ben, you don't know each other, but you all three are awesome coaches in your own field, and you have influenced me deeply. Thank you for your guidance and wisdom.

To Dusty, I love you for your friendship, support, and heartfelt reaction on my manuscript.

To all my clients and students, thank you for your trust. You have all inspired the second part of my book. You are living proof that if you live with passion, many things can be overcome, whether it's sexual abuse or other ordeals you have been through.

To the many dancers and dance teachers in the world who have reacted and supported me throughout the fundraising and promotion of this book, especially Barbara, Louis, Julie, Peter, Ton, Laura, Massimo, Joanna, Michael, Jukka, Sirpa, Neil, and Katja.

To all donors, without whom it would not have been possible to publish and promote this book in this timeframe.

To Rob and crew at Bestseller Publishing, whose unique publishing concept makes it possible to bring stories like mine to a large audience.

Last but certainly not least, a special thank you to Irene, my student and my friend. Your belief in my work, my teaching and my story, have helped me to finish this book and continue our work. You have edited my book, you have been by my side to raise the necessary funds to publish and promote it, and you were there to start A Dancer's Movement to Stop Sexual Abuse. I will never be able to fully express how grateful I am for all your efforts. I'll always love you for this and for just being who you are.

Made in USA - Kendallville, IN
1220160_9781790476381
12 30 2020 1128